IMAGES OF ENGLAND

South Croydon, Selsdon and Sanderstead

In 1917, this Briton Hill farm scene would have been equally commonplace in Selsdon, Croham and even in the Haling Manor area of South Croydon. There were always fields 'beneath' any urban or suburban development.

IMAGES OF ENGLAND

South Croydon, Selsdon and Sanderstead

Ralph Rimmer

NONSUCH

Around 1905, it was possible to walk along a country lane to reach the Croham Hurst beauty spot and then to look back across farm fields to Croydon.

This book is dedicated to the members of the Selsdon Camera Club, past and present, who have shared their skills and friendship with me.

First published 1997
This new pocket edition 2005
Text and images unchanged from first edition

Nonsuch Publishing Limited
The Mill, Brimscombe Port,
Stroud, Gloucestershire, GL5 2QG
www.nonsuch-publishing.com

British Library Cataloguing in Publication Data.
A catalogue record for this book is available from the British Library.

ISBN 1-84588-107-9

Typesetting and origination by Nonsuch Publishing Limited.
Printed in Great Britain by Oaklands Book Services Limited.

Contents

Godfrey Talbot LVO OBE, is a man of many talents who has won wide national acclaim as well as local respect in the Croydon area. He is noted as a journalist who has worked on *The Guardian* and for twenty-five years he was the Court Correspondent. As a broadcaster he has been a radio cricket commentator, as well befits a Yorkshire man, and has been an interpreter of royal occasions on both radio and television. He is the author of a number of books on the royal family. Although he has had national and international commitments, for example, with the Royal Overseas League, he has always found time to respond to requests for his services in the local area. For a number of years he was President of the Sanderstead Preservation Society and has been a worthy advocate for local heritage issues.

In 1983 Godfrey Talbot lent his official invitation to the Coronation of Queen Elizabeth II to an exhibition in All Saints' Church, Sanderstead.

Introduction

One is tempted to say that Dr Rimmer is misnamed, for what he never does is touch merely the *rim* or edge or surface of things. Only deep research is Ralph's accomplished way. Modest and unassuming though his character may be, he is nevertheless a tiger when it comes to the deep pursuit of a telling photograph.

I am honoured to essay a few words of introduction to this new book formed by his pages of pictures and prose that can bring life and historic animation to some agreeable outposts of suburban Surrey, well south of London and indeed, below skyscraper Croydon and verging towards forests and downland.

I write as a moorland north-countryman who has, however, lived half by town and half by down in Sanderstead (Ralph's own suburb) for half a century of war and peace. So it is a joy to look at this compilation of places and people, buildings and boundaries, delightfully captured by photographers, amateur and professional, past and present. This anthology of images has been carefully collected, thoughtfully selected and then meticulously copied and printed in the Rimmer darkroom.

To call the publication 'local history' is not at all belittling Ralph's gallery presented here, for this book, I think, lures far beyond geography; it would touch my own heartstrings whether I was on a bench in Croham Hurst or a bus breaching Chorlton-cum-Hardy.

There is a mixture of snapshot and camera-craft, of reminiscence and history – and much more – in the following pages. These are photographs to be enjoyed in their scanning over and over again.

Godfrey Talbot LVO OBE

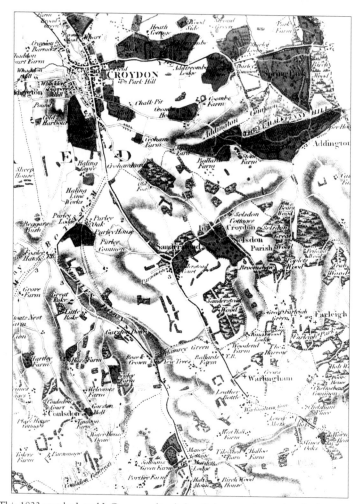

This 1823 map by J. and I. Greenwood includes all the areas depicted in this book. Travelling south along the main Brighton Road to the district around the Haling Lime Works is illustrated in Section One. The country routes to Croham Hurst, Croham Farm and Old Fox Farm are considered in Section Two. Section Three portrays the Selsdon Parish and its woods. Section Four involves the Purley Oaks, Purley Common and Riddlesdown localities. Sections Five, Six and Seven describe the Sanderstead neighbourhood as far as Sanderstead Wood and Hamsey Green. The book is designed to show the development of the area arising from the manorial estates of Haling, Croham and Sanderstead, which included Selsdon and Purley Bury estates.

One

South End to Windsor Castle

It was always a pleasure when travelling to the southern districts around Croydon to gaze on the magnificent Grand Theatre, even though it had lost the grandeur of its august external appearance long before its demolition in 1959. The Grand Theatre, which stood between the Wrencote building and Nalder and Collyer's brewery, was opened as the New Grand Opera House on 6 April 1896, by Sir Herbert Beerbohm Tree. He brought his Haymarket Theatre players to perform the play *Trilby* in the opening week. Great artistes like Sarah Bernhardt, Mrs Patrick Campbell and Ellen Terry appeared there, although latterly the theatre was better known for its splendid pantomimes.

In this 1916 photograph, the most prominent feature is the large chimney on the left. It had been built as part of John Cooper's boot and shoe factory (see page 19). When Cooper moved his factory to Northampton the premises were used for the printing works of the *Surrey Morning and Evening Echo*. From 1894 the buildings were used as a warehouse and, as Ebbutt's Furniture Repository, were demolished in the 1980s.

The Blue Anchor Inn, 41 South End, shown here in about 1914, was first mentioned in about 1644 at Haling (see page 15). Originally a stream ran by it and there was a tollgate nearby. On the right of the picture once stood Blunt House, the home of Sir Gilbert Scott who designed St Pancras station in London and St Peter's Church in South Croydon (see page 30).

In 1903, this was the third building of the Swan and Sugar Loaf Inn. Originally it was a farmhouse of the Archbishop of Canterbury whose symbols, a mitre (resembling a sugar-loaf hat) and a crozier, (a bent crook like the curve of a swan's neck), gave the name to the inn. Thomas Tilling's horse-drawn buses, each carrying twelve passengers, parked on the forecourt and there was stabling for the horses at the rear.

The Swan and Sugar Loaf, c. 1910, was proud of its red plush and gilded fitments which were supplied by the owners, Page and Overton, a Croydon brewery. The Union Jack Co. buses, shown here, were in operation from 1905 and the indicators show that they travelled to Oxford Circus through Thornton Heath, Norbury and Streatham. In 1901 a main line electric tramway service was opened for service between Norbury and Purley and closed in 1951.

Left: This bookmark souvenir was given to patrons of the Central Hall Picture Palace to commemorate the Coronation of George V in 1911. The cinema began its life in 1910 as the Swan Electric Theatre. When James Watt took over in 1911, he renamed it Central Hall to match the rest of his cinema chain as, for example, the Central Cinema in Catford. Latterly Mr Watts had a house built in Beechwood Road, Sanderstead, which is now a rest-home. In 1927 the cinema became the Dome and in 1932 the Savoy. Its final manifestation was as the Classic Cinema, between 1934 and 1973, surviving a number of alterations of name and policy until its closure. (See *The Cinemas of Croydon*, Eyles and Skone, 1989).

Below: In the middle of the souvenir there was a piece of cine film. When held to the light it was possible to see this exterior view of the cinema.

Opposite above: The Croydon Bowling Club can trace its ancestry to 1749 when bowls was played behind the Three Tuns Inn, near the Parish Church. The game continued to be played there until 1907 when the inn was demolished. Until 1920 the club continued its activities at a ground off the High Street before moving to its present site in Nottingham Road. Here an outdoor match is in progress in 1938.

The club-room in 1938, just before it and the croquet lawn were developed in that year. Further expansion occurred in 1965, which linked the old club-house with the indoor pavilion providing spacious dressing rooms, a lounge bar, a TV room and a board and general meeting room. Today its premises are palatial, yet still retain a welcoming and relaxed atmosphere for bowling and social events. The club's archives are currently being processed for a history to be published in 1999 to celebrate its 250th Anniversary.

The Croydon Bowling Club Board at the time of the Indoor Section's 50th Anniversary in 1981. Back row, from left to right: Mrs P. Ward, F. Sewell, W. Alford, P. Dunkley, Mrs E. Buckland, C. Wells. Front row: R. Adamson (Treasurer), R. Gwilliam (Vice-President), G. Kirk (President), H. Sendall (Secretary).

An EBA Indoor Section international match in progress on 25 February 1939, in the indoor pavilion that was opened in October 1937. In the Second World War the War Ministry took over the club premises and a heavy consignment of goods left on the indoor playing area resulted in a 'big swing' on Rink 2 - at least some members think so! Over the years a good number of the members has achieved international honours for this proud club.

Haling House in 1896, with Col James Watney II mounted. The Watney family had acquired its wealth through the Croydon banking firm of Watney, Moore and Smith and a later association with the Watney brewery firm. After he had led the defeat of the Armada, Haling Manor was given to Admiral Effingham by Queen Elizabeth I, who created him Earl of Nottingham. Sheep and cattle were permitted to graze in the lower park, after the weekly cattle market, until the butchers required them.

By 1930, the Whitgift Estate had acquired most of the Haling Manor Estate. In 1931 the Whitgift School moved from its buildings in North End and took up its new premises at Haling Park. On 8 July 1931, Prince George, Duke of Kent, officially opened the school and reviewed the Officers' Training Corps. From left to right: A.J. Camden-Field (Chairman of the Governors), the Mayor of Croydon, Capt F.H. Potter, Lord Ashcombe (Lord Lieutenant of the County) and Prince George.

As well as having an outstanding academic record, Whitgift School is also justifiably proud of its sporting achievements. This was Whitgift School's First Cricket XI in 1971. Back row, from left to right: Tarrett, Hughes, Mr Branston, Alexander, Townsend and Moore. Front row: Chinnock, Perrott, Ryan (Captain), Wordsworth, Stone and Powell.

In 1967, Whitgift School won the Public Schools Seven-a-side Competition. Held aloft is C.D. Saville (Captain) and the others are, from left to right: Nesbitt, Paterson, Freter, Bloxham, Skeen and Malempre. Gerwyn Williams, the Welsh international, trained this successful team.

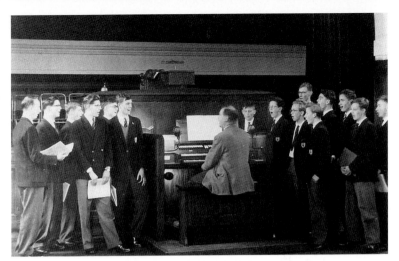

Director of Music, John S. Odom, rehearsing the school choir in 1971. His first appointment was as part-time Director of Music with mathematics as a second teaching area. In recognition of his outstanding work with the corps of drums, choir and orchestra, he was made the school's first full-time Director. In collaboration with Ian F. Smith he produced memorable performances of operettas and operas.

In January 1980, Mr F.R. Pattison showed participant encouragement to young Whitgift cyclists. From left to right: Bates, Churchill-Coleman, Hilliard, M. Hilliard, S. Stephenson, Mr Pattison, Miller (half-hidden), Montrioux, Hubbard, Colville, Maxwell, Mayes, Symes, Love, Besden-Smith, Strenies, Brown, Edmonds, Scott, Wilkinson, Parsons, Davis, Curtis and Karpal.

The chimneys of Haling Park Cottage were clearly visible across the forecourt of Davis's wood yard in Brighton Road in the First World War, c. 1917. The Albion motor lorry was, however, a pre-war product. The Davis timber yard was well established by 1907 at 85 Brighton Road, situated next to Hyde's Nurseries. Steam-driven sawmills had also been introduced by 1914.

The South Croydon Baptist Church was built in about 1893 on land bought from James Watney. From the 1860s, services acceptable to Baptists and other denominations had been held in the cottages of William Pressey and Mrs Bucknell. The district had been evangelized by Walter Schwind, encouraged by Emily Watney, from a mission hall in Purley Downs Road. The development of a separate Baptist church was promoted by Charles Haddon Spurgeon, the great Baptist preacher. The first minister in 1894 was the Reverend H.J. Milledge, after whom the Milledge Memorial Sunday School was named in his honour (See *The Non-Conformist Experience in Croydon*, J. Morris, 1992.).

In this 1933 Brighton Road scene, the Milledge Memorial building is clearly visible. The shop to the right of Drewett's, W.H. Pain, was well known for its cold meat and faggots. This was the last shop before Tilling's bus garage. The boy, front left, is almost walking out of the picture in his eagerness either to go to S.H. White's below or, perhaps, to the Purley Oaks School, on the following page.

Although the original photograph of S.H.White's newsagents at 277 Brighton Road is marked '1914' on the reverse, the shop does not appear in directories until 1928. There had been few shops in Brighton Road (constructed between 1805 and 1816) until the end of the nineteenth century. Most of the buildings in Brighton Road were cottages or villas. In Bynes Road, to the right of S.H. White's cottages, John Cooper built thirty-eight houses and three shops for the employees at his boot and shoe factory (see page 10). They were numbered between 103 and 179. Locally they received the title of 'Snob's Island'.

The new Purley Oaks School was built just prior to the Second World War and as it was ready, opened in 1940, although in September 1939, 148 children had left with Mr Oliver and thirteen of the staff for evacuation to Crowborough, Maresfield, Forest Row and Framfield. The old building, originally called Brighton Road School and seen here in the background, opened in 1873. It was one of the first schools to be built in response to the 1870 Education Act. The immediate area of the school was undeveloped at the time. Bynes Road had just seven houses and only Napier Road was built up, with fifty-two houses. Brighton Road on the far side from the school was given to farming.

Pupils of the Brighton Road Girls' School in 1899, including Mabel, Edith and Ethel White. The school did not become known as Purley Oaks until 1922.

A Brighton Road School infants' class in 1920. Mary Boughey was headteacher of the infants' school from about 1902 until 1921. When the school was reorganised she became the head of the juniors and infants until 1926.

Probably one of the last Brighton Road School's boys-only classes in about 1921. From 1922, when the school became Purley Oaks, both senior school and junior school classes became mixed. In 1922 Mr Lambourne, who had been the school's first pupil teacher, retired after forty-nine years of service to the school, which included thirty-four years as headteacher.

In this picture of the Purley Oaks School football team, around 1926, it may be noted that the boys were all correctly attired. The necks of their jerseys were drawn tightly with laces, as was the fashion. The members of staff were also formally dressed and the one on the right, perhaps the headteacher, was wearing a bow tie and spats to cover his shoe-laces. In 1923, a year in which the teachers went on strike, their average annual salary was about £150 for men and about £112 for women. Male headteachers received between £440 and £600, but female headteachers received only between about £350 and £480.

In the season 1955/1956 the Purley Oaks' netball team triumphantly displayed its winners' trophy. These team members were among the junior school children who witnessed the departure of the senior school members in 1955 to South Croydon Secondary School (now Haling Manor High School). Miss Iris Maynard then became the head of the junior school from 1955 to 1976.

The Purley Oaks School football team of 1955/1956 played in the Croydon Junior Schools' League. Home matches were played on Purley Oaks Recreation Ground.

The Purley Oaks School's athletics team of 1960 competed at the Croydon Sports Arena. Miss Maynard, headteacher, was one of the main organisers of the Borough Schools Athletics meetings.

At the turn of the century this area was known as Purley Bottom. Even in the 1920s it retained some of its rural origins. There was a cow yard on the corner of Crunden Road and cattle were taken along Brighton Road for grazing near where Avondale Road now stands. The Red Deer was originally built in 1847 as a beer house on open space near Gallows Green, where James Cooper, a highwayman, was hanged in 1749. The present building was erected by Mr Bullock, a local builder. The forecourt of the Red Deer was used as a bus terminus until 1950.

A veteran car just passing a 1968 Mini estate, near the Purley Arms, during the London to Brighton run, c. 1970. The first number-plate issued in Croydon was BY 74. Reg and Fred Miles, owners of Onwood Motors by the Red Deer, were keen veteran car enthusiasts. Onwood Motors was one of the first buildings in Croydon to generate its own electricity. Originally Onwood Motors had belonged to their parents and was also associated with bicycles. A flying bomb destroyed the premises in 1944 but the business restarted in 1949, and many local motorists received their instruction at the Onwood Driving School.

On 18 June 1927, Major General Sir Edward Woodward opened the garden
fête of St Augustine's Church. By his side was the vicar, the Revd E. Moore.
St Augustine's Church was designed by the architect J. Oldrid Scott, son of Sir
Gilbert Scott, who designed St Peter's Church (See page 30). The Archbishop
of Canterbury consecrated St Augustine's in 1884 and the architect donated the
clock from Blunt House, where he had lived as a child (See page 10). The new
parish took in part of the Sanderstead parish below the Oxted railway line.

A staff versus school cricket match was held at South Croydon Secondary School
on 24 July 1957. Front row, from left to right: Mr Saunders, Mr Gosling, Mr de
Voil (headteacher), Mr C. Hansford, Mr Ashdown, Mr Green, Mr Alexander
(caretaker). Others present were: Mr Fruin, Mrs Hibbit, Mr Bacon, Miss Colwell,
Miss West, Miss Davies, Mrs Ranzetta (?), Miss Sabin (?), Miss Watts, Mr
Morgan. From 1970, a merger of South Croydon Secondary School with Croydon
Secondary Technical School resulted in the present Haling Manor High School.

This was how Brighton Road, near Purley Arms, looked in 1928. At the time the Funnell family had a tradition as landlords of the Purley Arms. In 1882 there were few shops in this area. Brighton Cottages were situated between the Red Deer and the Purley Arms and from there to the Windsor Castle were only cottages and villas. By 1928 it was possible to buy everything here from, for example, Baldwin's the butcher, Young's the draper and Coupe the jeweller. The rather ornate shop behind the people in the right foreground belonged to B.H. Trill and Son. The exterior of the shop retains some of the original ornamentation.

The name of Killick has been associated with 190 Brighton Road, as tobacconist, confectioner and newsagent since about 1915. The group posing in front of the shop must have been standing outside a fairly new shop as 'War Economy Tea' of the First World War was on sale. The name Killick, which sounds Celtic, has been long associated with Croydon. At least six local Killicks perished in the Great Plague of 1665.

Douglas Oxenham was home on leave in 1941 and grooming his beloved horses. The Oxenham family had horses at their farm, Pace's Farm, Riddlesdown, and at their stables in Helder Street. They hired horses out to local tradesmen. In the background is Mr Congram's cart. Congram's bakery had a bakehouse in Churchill Road and shops in Brighton Road and Cranleigh Parade, Sanderstead. Douglas Oxenham's father was the tenant farmer in Riddlesdown, whose father-in-law Charles Pace gave his name to the farm. Charles Pace became a master-builder and constructed 'Tansley' in Brighton Road for his daughter and son-in-law. His granddaughter, Dorothy, maintains the family home and its stables against all the development around her.

This float was prepared and festooned by Mr Oxenham for the Croydon Streets of Adventure event, in aid of Croydon General Hospital, in about 1937.

The Misses Blanche, newsagents, at 271 and 273 Brighton Road, published this postcard of Page and Overton's inn, the Windsor Castle. It was a stopping place for refreshment and shopping for mail coaches from London where horses could be changed. It may also have been a stopping place for coaches carrying mail to Windsor and its Castle, from which it may have derived its name. The Windsor Castle has held a licence for over 400 years. Doodlebugs in 1944 fell nearby, killing a number of people, including a boy cyclist.

In 1894 this cattle fair was held near the Windsor Castle. There were no houses on the opposite side of the road, the only houses being on the Purley Arms side. The cast-iron farm implements show how rural the community was. The cattle fair was held annually until 1931. Churchill Road now stands on the original site. (Photo: Predominantly Paper, 0181-667-1671)

Two

From South Croydon to Croham Hurst

O.J. Morris of Beulah Hill photographed the Victoria to Brighton express passing through South Croydon station on 8 October 1919. The station had been opened on 1 September 1865 for the London Brighton & South Coast Railway. Children referred to the company as the 'London Brighton Smash up and Turn Over Railway'. In contrast the South Eastern & Chatham Railway (SE&CR) was called the 'Slow Easy and Comfortable'. Its leisurely approach was emphasised by its custom of providing its stations with Bibles.

In 1849, the foundation stone of St Peter's Church, designed by Sir George Gilbert Scott of Blunt House, was laid by G.R. Smith Esq. of Selsdon House (See page 42). It was consecrated in 1851, the year of the Great Exhibition and the opening of a new cattle market in South Croydon. The church stood on the brow of a hill in splendid isolation, overlooking fields. Its dominating spire was a gift from a blind lady, Eleanor Rohde, who was said to have died in poverty but who is commemorated in the church. The spire was burnt down in 1864 but was soon restored. In the 1920s a small school was attached to the church, where Mr Chote, the caretaker, made coke fires and was dearly loved by the children. A bomb blast in 1944 destroyed the school. At the same time, the verger lost his wife, daughter and grandchild in the raid.

In 1891, these children were in Archbishop Tennison's School, which from 1852 was situated near to where St Peter's Church was built. Tennison's was founded in 1714 and occupied the site where Debenham's is in North End today. In 1959 the school moved to Selborne Road.

The cars and the presence of a wireless (radio) shop suggest that this was the Selsdon Road scene, near the Swan and Sugar Loaf, in the late 1920s or early 1930s. Many people at the time had battery radios or ones that needed accumulators, which had to be collected from a radio shop and returned for recharging. The ornamental gables on the shops on the far right in Ledbury Terrace gave them the name of the 'Swiss Houses'. Hyde, the florist and seedsman, has had a presence on the left side of the road for over a century. Selsdon Road itself had its origins in mediaeval times. It was a route to Selesdune/ Sellesdon/ Selsdon when the manorial lands belonged to the Knights Templar Crusaders. In the eighteenth century Selsdon Road was a country lane called Brechefield Road, where it was hazardous to walk alone because of highwaymen. Later, with all the farms and estates around it, the lane was a poacher's paradise.

Prominent in this photograph is the building to the left labelled 'Ye Market'. It was No. 12 of the twelve shops in the row. In 1899 Mr Mills, chemist, and a lady photographer were the first occupants of No. 12. From 1906 it belonged to Nobles, father and son, who were also chemists and persisted in the use of some of the earliest utensils. In 1997 as the Old Imperial Pharmacy, the shop lay empty. The Croham Arms inn, to the right, was under construction during 1865/6 and became a house of Nalder & Son, a Croydon brewery. On the opposite side of Selsdon Road, near Cliffe Road, was the Stag and Hounds inn, which had its own livery stables. The name of the inn was probably derived from an 1877 landlord, James Roffey, a huntsman to the stag-hounds. He is buried in St Peter's churchyard.

On the same side of the road as the Stag and Hounds was the Surrey Drovers inn, seen here on the right in 1904. The cattle market off Selsdon Road, opened in 1848, was the largest in the south of England. Cattle were brought from up to ten miles away. Few roads had been built at that time and many were unsafe for travellers. Many farmers had to wait to return the following day, hence the large number of inns in the vicinity. The Surrey Drovers at No. 54 was next door to the livery stables of Timothy Graves. At No. 64 there was a dairy farm, and at No. 72 was Roff's slaughterhouse and stables.

The newly-erected St Emmanuel's Church, 1902, was built in 1899 in the Decorated Style. Everything about the church was dignified and simple so that, for example, the choir did not wear surplices. When first opened, the church had clear views over Croydon and Purley and the rear overlooked Croham Farm. The church's philosophy was to reach out to its parishioners and others. It had a football and a cricket team and promoted charities, such as that for the poor mothers of Battersea.

The Misses Watney provided the money for building Emmanuel Church, which managed to survive the damage inflicted by flying bombs in 1944. Right is Miss Emily Watney, photographed by Elliott and Fry of Baker Street, in about 1880. She lived with her sister, Alice, in a modest house at 101 Selsdon Road, called Sunny Nook. They were the daughters of James Watney I of Haling Manor and they lived their Christianity through their daily giving of themselves. They provided full-time nurses, Nurse Jeffries and Nurse Coomber, as workers among poor women of the area and to provide a free midwifery service. The Misses Watney also attended on the mothers in their homes. Alice Watney died in 1917 but Emily survived until 1932. A member of Emily's Bible class said that he wished he had died at the same time as she did because the gates of heaven would have been opened so wide that even he might have crept in.

Haling Road Hall, South Croydon.

The Misses Watney also provided for Haling Road Hall as a Sunday school for local children.

On 10 August 1885, the Woodside and South Croydon Railway opened this station as Selsdon Road. The railway bridge in Selsdon Road marked the extent of urban development in Croydon. War economies brought about its closure in the First World War, but it reopened in 1919 as Selsdon station. The photograph shows a steam train in 1948. Steam persisted on the line until the 1950s. Selsdon had been the junction for Woodside and Elmers End and provided a link with Kent and an alternative route to London's Charing Cross station. All the station buildings were removed in 1977 and the line was finally closed in 1983.

The buildings on the left in 1924, probably the dwellings of farm workers, would have been seen by visitors as they left Selsdon station and made their way along an unmade track to Croham Hurst. The cottages were replaced by modern residences when the road was widened. Visitors would also have seen a more magnificent abode from the path. This was Croham Hurst House, built in the early nineteenth century. After several tenants had moved in and out after only a brief tenancy, the house became the property of the Kemmis family. The final member of the family to live there was Captain A.H.N. Kemmis, who died in 1918. The house, which has three wells in its ground, still stands but is no longer so open to the public gaze.

Old Fox Farm in 1921 had reached the end of arable farming and by 1924 had been taken over by Welford's Dairy, which was eventually merged into United Dairies. Old Fox did not feature on maps as a farm until 1843. The buildings were probably originally those of an inn, into whose well in 1758 Elizabeth Stagg had fallen and drowned. She was buried in All Saints' churchyard in Sanderstead.

This narrow lane, in about 1920, just wide enough for a wagon, was called Old Fox Path and still runs between Beechwood Road and West Hill. Originally it continued across fields to Purley. The Footpath Preservation Society's attempt to save its full length was turned down officially because the path was claimed to be for entry to fields and not for use as a public footpath. Local people had, however, used the path extensively to reach Purley station. The names of fields on the Fox Farm have been preserved in the names of local roads, including Barnfield Close and Day's Acre.

This view of Fox Farm shows the narrowness of the tracks that led from Selsdon station to the village of Selsdon and to the Old Fox Path. Croham Hurst was to the right of the track. Towards the middle of the nineteenth century the owner of Old Fox Farm appears to have abandoned the old farmhouse in favour of the timber-clad house which is now at No. 211 Upper Selsdon Road. The area around was worked as a farm.

Past the footpath to Sanderstead Church, marked on maps, there were, on the right of the Selsdon way, four Fox Farm cottages. Some cottages on the estate were taken down in 1926 and the cottages shown here were in the process of demolition in 1935.

Before ascending Croham Hurst, these young ladies might have partaken of some light refreshments at a wooden hut, at about 442 Upper Selsdon Road. This was called Boundary Store and was outside Old Fox Farm.

In about 1920 the countryside spreading out to the rear of these youthful visitors gave no hint of the housing estates to be built there. The boys appear to be attempting to hide from view. Like generations of children before and after, they may have been listening for or looking for turtle-doves, jays, tree-creepers, cuckoos, squirrels, weasels or moles. The wild life there was abundant and, in 1901, twenty-six species of fungus could be found. Today there are still pleasing views when looking from the same position because the houses are hidden by a profusion of trees. As one looks towards All Saints' Church, Sanderstead, in its dominating position, it is a view common to local dwellers for almost 800 years.

View from Croham Hurst looking over
Croham Farm, St Paul's Presbyterian
Church, Emmanuel Church and, in the
far distance, the Crystal Palace, in 1920.
After the Great Exhibition of 1851 the
Crystal Palace was moved to Sydenham,
where it continued to attract visitors
and observers from Croham Hurst, until
it was burnt down in 1936. On the
Hurst itself, the barrows are a scheduled
ancient monument of Bronze age men
of about 2000 BC, whose religion
required them to bury their dead. Other
evidence has arisen from time to time
to suggest even earlier habitation and
an examination of two hut sites here in
1968 claims habitation on the site 7,000
years ago!

Croham Farm nestled below 'the cliffs of an old sea beach' and was situated where the Old
Whitgiftians' playing fields are today. In 1894 Croham Manor Road was just a bridle road
between Croham Farm and Croham Hurst House. When Croham Manor Road was first
built in about 1911, residents had to walk through the farm to take the train from Spencer
Road Halt, another station that closed for war economies in the First World War.

The Croham Hurst Golf Club in the 1920s was in a distinctly rural setting, yet only 12 miles from London. Thrift Wood, with its Early Purple Orchids and Butterfly Orchids lay within its bounds. In 1952, full members had to pay an entrance fee of about £10.50 and an annual subscription was about £14.70. It was a fee worth paying because Harry Weetman was the club professional.

The Croham Hurst golf course was laid out by the 'great' James Braid and was not the easiest of courses. It was 6,077 yards around and the first two holes, of 473 yards and 443 yards, both finished uphill. The club-house must have appeared very relaxing with its Lloyd Loom chairs. These were similar to those used in the cabins on the Imperial Airways Croydon to Paris air service. In the seventeenth century, near to the site of the club-house, there used to be a piped spring.

St Paul's Presbyterian Church had been part of the scene from 1905. The church had been designed by the architect of Croydon Town Hall, Charles Henman. In 1907 Castlemaine Avenue was in course of erection, followed in 1908 by Melville Avenue. The big house on the right became Croham Hurst School.

CROHAM HURST SCHOOL, SOUTH CR

Croham Hurst School was founded in 1899 by Miss Kathleen Ellis. By the time that this aerial photograph was taken in 1935, the school had been enlarged to provide extensive facilities. In 1951 it became a public school. School loyalty had already been engendered by 1911, when the school's annual reunion on the last Saturday in June was so well attended by Old Crohamians. Its first joint presidents were its founder Miss Ellis, and its first Principal, Miss Theodora Clark. Their names will, no doubt, be to the fore when the school celebrates its Centenary in 1999.

Three

Selsdon

In 1902, this platinotype photograph was taken by P.H. Mason of Croydon Camera Club. It shows the fields that used to be where the village now stands. The ancient estate of Selsdon (Selesdune: the hill of Seles) was part of the Manor of Sanderstead and was among the eighteen hides given to the Abbey of Hyde in Winchester by Ethelfleda, wife of Edgar and mother of Edward the Confessor. At the Dissolution of the Monasteries, the estate was rented by Sir John Gresham, whose grandson sold Selsdon to John Ownstead (the Younger). In 1676 Selsdon Park was owned by Christopher Bowyer, who is buried in Sanderstead churchyard. Until 1883 Selsdon was part of Croydon Crook, and from 1894 to 1915 part of Croydon Rural District Council, until joining the Urban District Council of Coulsdon and Purley. In 1900 it was a tiny hamlet of seventeen cottages and forty people; by 1953 the population had increased to 7,000.

In the eighteenth century Selsdon consisted of a mansion, parkland, a farm, farm labourers and much woodland. The main route from Croydon through Selsdon was, in part, an Iron Age track, which continued to Titsey along a track across the present Selsdon Park. The present pseudo-Tudor building was mostly completed by William Coles in 1809 and possibly extended by George Smith, who landscaped the gardens. His son, George Robert Smith MP, further developed it. When the Sanderson family took over from Wickham Noakes in 1923, a twenty-four bedroom hotel was established which, under their care, became a 160 room hotel and conference centre. Its latest owners have plans to increase the accommodation by another 100 bedrooms.

In 1880 the only two listed Selsdon residents were the Bishop of Rochester, who rented Selsdon Park, and William Langford, a farmer. The latter was at Selsdon Farm which, here in 1920, stood in isolation. When George Smith rebuilt his Selsdon Park mansion and reorganised his estate, he also erected this new farm with cottages in Addington Road (c. 1815-1820). The site became a supermarket. The Good Neighbour public house, now called the Stag, replaced the farm cottages.

A 1927 aerial view of Costain's development of Selsdon. The first house had been built in 1923 in Byron Road. A 1927 advertisement showed that some of the new houses were being sold for £650. As a comparison, Selsdon Park was sold for £13,000 in 1924. St Mary's Church Hall may be seen standing on its own in a field along Upper Selsdon Road. There were few other amenities. As a contemporary remarked, 'All the first residents had were themselves.' The nearest school and post office were in Sanderstead. The nearest commuter station and public house were in South Croydon, a two mile walk.

The builder's caption to this 1920s photograph states that it was where Queenhill Road became Farley Road but local historian, Ted Frith, thinks that it was another Costain estate. The local council encouraged the development by giving a £75 subsidy per house to the builder, Costain, a Liverpool Manxman. In Farley Road, Croham Valley Road, Littleheath Road and Brent Road, 1,000 houses were offered at £425 each. Mortgages would have cost about £30 down and £3 monthly repayment. In 1926 Farley Road was opened fully and became a major route to Croydon.

Foxearth Road and Rylands Road were under construction from the mid-1920s. In 1926 there were just eight houses on the south side and by 1928, there were twenty-eight houses altogether.

The car standing alone in Foxearth Road suggests that the photograph was taken in the early 1930s. Most people in that era had to use public transport. In 1925 the only means of reaching South Croydon for the morning trains was on the free bus provided by Costain's. Problems arose from overcrowding when lonely housewives used the free bus to meet their husbands from South Croydon station. An East Surrey Traction Co. bus service, prompted by the ever lively Selsdon Residents Association, replaced the free bus. It ran at 30 minute intervals to and from Croham Heights (Selsdon Park lodge gates). The bus was numbered 417 and cost 2d (about 1p) to South Croydon. The LTA introduced the No. 54 bus in 1927 and the No. 234 bus in 1949.

In 1926, Costain's were using a narrow gauge railway in Farley Road, similar to the little railways of Wales. Farley Road was initially built from the crossroads to Queenhill Road and was not completed until 24 July 1926.

Farley Road still had the appearance of an unmade surface in this postcard, sent in 1930. The car in the foreground suggests that the photograph, taken by W.H. Drake, photographer, of No. 2 Ecclesbourne Road, Thornton Heath, was exposed in about 1928.

The earliest recorded Anglican services in Selsdon were taken by the Rector of Sanderstead, the Revd Graham Jones, in a shepherd's hut. Building of a temporary church hall began in February 1927. In 1934 this plan for a permanent church, St John the Divine, was on public view. In October 1935 the foundation stone of the new church was laid by Miss Alice Warner.

In 1936 the Revd Cyril Wayneforth, seen here with his family, worked tirelessly for a permanent church in Selsdon. He was also determined to see the emergence and development of a social life and fellowship among his congregation, especially among children and young people.

The Revd Cyril Wayneforth had been appointed as a priest-in-charge of the church hall but when the ambition of a permanent church was realised in 1936, he became the vicar. The final service in the church hall was held on 11 October 1936. In the following week, on 17 October, the new church was consecrated by the Archbishop of Canterbury. Seven hundred people were present at the service. Revd Cyril Wayneforth remained as vicar until 1948 and guided the church through the war period.

Another Archbishop of Canterbury, Geoffrey Fisher, visited the church on Saturday 15 October 1955, on the occasion of the installation of the Revd Ewart Roberts BA RNVR, as Perpetual Curate of St John the Divine Church, Selsdon.

Some members of Selsdon Camera Club provided photographs of St John the Divine Church for display during its Diamond Jubilee year in 1996. The club also puts on an exhibition to support the church's summer fair. One member of the club, Vic Smith, a consulting structural engineer and a respected architectural photographer, made a unique montaged photograph of the church using a hundred pieces of coloured photographs, which he had carefully cut and matched. The final version was presented to Selsdon Camera Club to mark its 50th Anniversary in 1997. The club then offered it to the church during a special service as a mark of the close relations enjoyed over many years. This black and white copy cannot do full justice to the glory of the coloured original, but fortunately the framed montage is on permanent display in the church.

Opposite above: In early October 1940, plans were published for procedures in the event of an air raid during services. Fortunately the actual raid occurred outside wartime service hours. At 8.30 pm on 26 October 1940, there was a direct hit on the church. Another bomb destroyed the church hall. The Baptist Church and the tennis club were quick off the mark to offer alternative premises.

Opposite below: The organ was badly damaged by the bombing but despite the disaster, a resilient congregation continued to worship in the mutilated building with temporary covers. By 1942 it was possible to hold a recital by the international pianist, Franz Wagner. In the same year Selsdon Choral Society and the church choir performed Mendelsohn's *Hymn of Praise*.

Above: Some of the members of Selsdon Camera Club in the 1997-1998 season when the club's 50 years of existence was celebrated. The club was formed in March 1946.

Left: Eric Maynard was the soul of the Selsdon Camera Club. He served as Treasurer for some twenty-five years and was always the first to arrive at the club and the last to leave, and always ensured that there was a good cup of tea for everyone in the interval. He maintained the club's links with the church where he assisted as a server for many years, and at one time was the organiser of the summer fair. He was the first member of the club to be honoured as its Life President.

Brian Ottaway was the heart of the Selsdon Camera Club. He served as Chairman through a number of difficult years and guided its emergence as one of the leading camera clubs in south London. His philosophy was that the next person to enter the club door as a prospective member was to be seen as its most important member. The club has continued, in the spirit of Eric Maynard and Brian Ottaway, to develop its status, with members and the club itself winning regional, national and international awards, whilst retaining its reputation for friendliness.

The Selsdon men's rambling club took its weekly walk in the 1980s and has continued doing so to this day. Several camera club members were in the group, including Fred Sinclair, Andrew Alexander and Len Topple. One of the members of the group, seen here near the centre, was Dr Alec Bookless, an inveterate walker, who came to Selsdon in 1938 and for fifty years served its community as a general medical practitioner. He is also energetic in securing a supply of medical equipment to the Third World.

As most of the newcomers to the Selsdon Garden 'Honeymoon' Village were newlyweds who were keen to start families, it soon became apparent that the village school in Sanderstead would be unable to cope with the growing numbers of children. In May 1928 a tin hut school with sixty-four children, aged from 5 to 10, commenced. By September 1931 the older parts of the present building were opened for senior and primary children with 189 children. By 1946 there were 432 children. In 1958 the Riddlesdown High School opened with 230 children and in 1965, Selsdon Senior School closed and its pupils were transferred there.

In the late 1930s, pupils of the Selsdon schools performed *A Midsummer Night's Dream*.

In 1938, pupils of Selsdon Primary School presented the pantomime *Dick Whittington*. Some of the players are, no doubt, now watching their grandchildren in school performances.

When Margaret Findlay was headteacher in 1949, the school held its 21st birthday party. A celebratory cake was made and the first slice was cut by the school's first headteacher, Dorothy Almond. Many former pupils returned to join in the festivities.

Class 2 performed a Nativity play in December 1962.

The Selsdon Primary School football team, 1956-1957. Back row, from left to right: T. Wood, R. Godfrey(?), P. Osborn, J. Nash, H. Springett, C. Onslow. Front row: T. Bonley(?), R. Davis, B. Boniface, I. Dollimore, G. Stevens.

The 1958-1959 Selsdon Primary School football team. Back row, from left to right: K. Belli, B. Wilkinson, M. Dale, P. Argent. Middle row: S. Harrison, P. Murton, J. Wotton, I. MacLachlan, A. Morgan. Front, seated: A. Wood, J. Burchett.

In about 1960, children from Selsdon Primary School were permitted to indulge their excitement at a fall of snow.

The first Selsdon Public Library was opened in May 1936 in Langley Oaks, a large old house and, for a long time, the home of Henry Hooper. Langley Oaks Library closed when the present library opened in 1967. The thirst for reading in Selsdon could be judged from this sale of books from the Croydon Public Libraries that attracted such large numbers to Selsdon Hall. Gill Huder took the photograph.

In 1956 Addington Road did not have yellow lines along the road; parking was plentiful and available and shopping was a comparatively easy and pleasurable pastime. In about 1931 Ladygrove pig and poultry farm was at No. 14, selling vegetables, honey and goats' milk. A.J. Butcher managed the post office and a printing press, as well as being a newsagent, bookseller, circulating library and hardware merchant. Sainsbury's opened in February 1950 and Woolworth's in 1954 (Ted Frith); Monty, the baker, was there in 1938. By 1969 only Hubbard and Nash, ironmongers, Nash, greengrocers and Hearn the butcher, remained of the original shopkeepers.

This was how the hardware shop of Hubbard and Nash looked in 1936, at No. 145 Addington Road. Other shops in the Broadway in 1928 included: Welford's Surrey Dairies Ltd; Hearn and Son, butcher; Richards, chemist; Worth's tobacco, confectionery and post office and Marion England, hairdresser. (By kind permission of Mr Mike Little)

Members of the British Legion, veterans of the First World War, gave the salute in Addington Road in the 1930s.

The view from Littleheath Woods was photographed by Charles H. Price of 62 High Street, Croydon, from where he began to operate around 1926. Such woodland views have been deemed worthy of conservation by the devoted Littleheath Woods Preservation Society, which is currently carrying out a survey of local woods that include Gee Wood, Foxearth Wood and Queenhill Shaw, as well as Littleheath Woods.

Along the Old Farleigh Road is one of the three Selsdon Park lodges. It was situated on the corner of Kingswood Way and became known as 'Cosy Corner'. In the 1920s, Mrs Lane, the wife of the keeper, sold mineral waters and sweets from a side window.

Right: The official opening of Selsdon Woods and Nature Reserve took place in 1936. In 1986 Sir William Davies, the Lord Mayor of London (left) and Peter Macdonald, Mayor of Croydon, planted oak trees to mark the 50th Anniversary.

Below: Craftsmen took part in the 1995 Annual Forestry Fair at Selsdon Wood. Early in the last century William Cobbett, on one of his rural rides, praised the men of Selsdon Wood for their outstanding skill in woodcraft. At the fair some of the local people dressed in the clothes of their rustic ancestors. They were photographed by Audrey Wright LRPS of the Selsdon Camera Club, who made a series of photographic records of the event.

On 8 October 1927, a hunting party stood in front of the Selsdon Park Hotel. The Worcester Park Beagles met in the grounds.

In December 1948, a small guest of Selsdon Park Hotel reached up to touch the bananas growing in the hot-house. In post-war austerity Britain, the hotel grew nearly all its own fruit, flowers and vegetables, including fruit from five banana trees.

In 1938, in the last peacetime Christmas, Selsdon Park Hotel grandly laid out its Christmas buffet and its festive food sculpture.

The Air Raid Wardens of Post 68, who included Harold Hodges, Martin Pink and Jack White, posed here during a lull in their wartime duties. They had to contend with conventional bombs in the early part of the war and with doodlebugs and flying bombs towards the end in 1944. When the peace came they could relax and, on Friday 21 September 1945, they held a Victory dinner at Selsdon Park Hotel.

Horace Murch Hon. FRPS, who lived at No. 49 Farley Road and latterly at No. 17 Mountfield Close, Sanderstead, was one of the finest amateur pictorial photographers. His landscape photographs appeared on exhibition walls and in galleries throughout the world. His influence on pictorial photography was enhanced by his prolific writing in journals, from the humble *Selsdon Gazette* where he had a monthly column, to most of the major international photographic magazines. He is shown here in one of his best known roles as a photographic competition judge, where again he enjoyed an international reputation.

On 29 April 1934, Horace Murch photographed his daughter, Beryl, in Selsdon Wood. At the time she was a pupil at Croydon High School and she is now Mrs John Briggs.

Four

From Sanderstead Road to the Downs

By 1914 the building of houses in Sanderstead Road appeared complete as far as St Gertrude's Church (built 1903) to the extent of this picture. Many of the houses on the right have disappeared and entrances to small factories are in their place. In 1914, on the left side, Nos 1 to 13 were shops where it was possible to buy almost anything, including confectionery, fish, corn and meal, meat, groceries and photographic requisites. The shop at No. 59 was an off licence and remains so today. In 1882 only Albert Cottages, Nos 1 to 6 and Nos 1 to 7, on the right side existed. The builder, William Brooker, lived at No. 1. Sanderstead Road continued to Sanderstead Crossroads, when it became Sanderstead village. (Photo: Predominantly Paper, 0181-667-1671)

This photograph of about 1903 is full of animation. On the right a lady in a long coat pushes a bassinet towards South Croydon Recreation Ground, where a soldier, standing idly, looks across the road at a uniformed nanny pushing a canopied pram near the shops. A boy holding a push chair waits outside a shop. Two ladies stand gossiping on the pavement in front of the 'Bazaar'. In 1903 and 1904, Merrony and Turner owned the 'Bazaar' near Kensington Terrace but by 1905 it became known as 'Merrony Stores'. Two men are riding in a horse-drawn cart. Perhaps they have come from one of the Sanderstead farms. A number of farm labourers in these farms were in lodgings in and around Sanderstead Road. Under the bridge five people walk in the middle of the road – impossible today. Altogether a busy scene amidst semi-rural peace is depicted. (Photo: Predominantly Paper, 0181-667-1671)

South Croydon Recreation Ground, 1938, has changed little from the original 1895 playground area. On the 8½ acre field local sports matches took place and on summer evenings a band played in the stand near Wyche Road.

William de Pirelea bought lands from the Manor of Sanderstead and thus a variation of his name became the source of Purley Bury House, the down house of Sanderstead Court (See pages 100 and 101). Each owner of the Purley Bury estate had to provide the Lord of Sanderstead Manor with a fully caparisoned war-horse. During the Civil War in the seventeenth century, the house was occupied by Bradshaw, who signed the death warrant of Charles I. An eighteenth-century tenant, John Horne Tooke, supported the rebels in the American War of Independence. He became MP for the rotten borough of Old Sarum and caused a constitutional crisis when, as a Church of England cleric, he took his seat in the House of Commons. Purley Bury House has now been reconstructed into a block of flats.

PURLEY OAKS, NEAR CROYDON

In 1905, the lodge to Purley Bury House was situated near the entrance to Purley Oaks Farm, whose gateway is seen on the left. A strip of land from Sanderstead Road to Purley Oaks Farm was known as Gibbet's Green. Dick Townley (See page 110) remembered seeing an old gallows built into one of the barns. When the farm was demolished in the 1930s, he tried to buy the gallows at an auction but failed in his bid.

Left: In 1901, one of the great Purley Oaks was photographed by J.H. Baldock of the Croydon Natural History and Scientific Society. He placed his camera bag in the picture to give an idea of the height and girth of the trees. The pollard oaks, whic surrounded the farm, were traditionally said to be tl remains of a primitive forest.

Opposite above: On 5 November 1899, Purley Oaks station was opened with its first station master, William Catchpole. With the arrival of the railway line the local population had grown and there wer soon thirty-four trains running daily. Sanderstead Junior and Kindergarten School was opened in 190 to meet the educational needs of the new populace. Among its owners have been Miss Weisgerber (1913), Mr and Mrs Parris Alexander (1926) and Miss Whistler and Miss Christopherson (1949). None has served as long as its present Principal, Mrs Alison Barnes. In this photograph she is being congratulated by Sir Ambrose Keevil, Lord Lieutenant of Surrey, on 3 December 1956 on the occasion of the 50th Anniversary of the school. Th well-respected private school now has a history of over 90 years.

In 1923, only one side of Purley Oaks Road had been built. It was still possible for its resident to obtain milk direct from Mr Laxton at Purley Oaks Farm if they took their own jugs. In 192 an outbreak of foot and mouth disease in one of its fields led to the destruction of the herd and the end of farming there. Previously farmers at Purley Oaks had also kept sheep on Purle Downs. A sign of approaching urbanisation may be glimpsed in the background - one of the first buses may be seen travelling along Sanderstead Road.

Two pupils of the above school posed for a snapshot in 1956. On the right is Mary Cooper and on the left, Anthea Barnes. The latter is now Mrs Burrell and she is the Deputy Principal of the School.

In the 1930s, pupils of Miss Nancy Privett took part in a dance fantasy. Among the children in the performance were Jean and Joan Cuthbert, Aileen, Rosemary and Marie Murton and Clare and Anthea Woolrich. Only one boy's name appeared in the programme, Michael Brill.

In early post-war Britain, c. 1948, there were still fuel deprivations and rationing. Nancy Privett ('Girlie' White) designed a *tableau vivant* to illustrate parallel wartime privations. In this scene are Nancy Privett, Mrs Windus, David West, Jill Williams, Sue Fullard and David Windus.

In this *tableau* depicting wartime evacuation, designed by Molly Ibbetson, are Jill Williams, Shirley Hunt, Jennifer Crowley, Sue Fullard, Genitha and Mavis Howell. Many children in the South Croydon area had experienced evacuation twice – in the 1940s to escape the heavy bombing and again in 1944, when doodlebugs and flying bombs targeted a locality that lay between Croydon airport and the Kenley airbase.

From the inauguration of Sanderstead Dramatic Club, it was a major social force in the district. Its first production, *A Joint Household* in 1907, starred Ivy Alexander, aunt of Nancy Privett, whose family have given excellent service to the club over many years. Early plays were held in St Michael's Church, West Croydon, and in St Augustine's Church Hall. Local Sanderstead people worked very hard to provide a Memorial Hall to honour the heroes of the First World War. In 1923 Sanderstead's own hero, Commander A.F.B. Carpenter VC RN of Zeebrugge fame, was aptly chosen to open the hall in Purley Oaks Road. Dr Everington was President of the Dramatic Club from 1908 until 1938, when he was tragically killed in a motor accident. The club took part in the inaugural concerts to herald the opening of All Saints' Church Hall in 1956. At this annual dinner of the Dramatic Club in the 1950s, the President, Rodney Mander and Mrs Mander are in the centre. Others recognised include Ann Betty, Richard Roberts, Sheila Pope, Diana Dewsbury, Sue White and Norman and Marjorie Peet.

In 1915 the temporary St Mary's Church Hall had recently been enlarged to meet the needs of a growing population. The original hall had been built by Mr Parsley for under £393. The field in which it was built had been donated by the Arkwright estate and forestalled those who had wanted the church to be erected nearer to the station. The hut-church was approached from the muddy track that served as Purley Oaks Road. By 1926 St Mary's had matured into its own parish with its own vicar, the Revd C.E. Fisher, and with its own permanent church. Its architecture was based on a fourteenth-century style.

Purley Beeches, Sanderstead 404354

The charm of Purley Beeches found favour in the diary of Samuel Pepys as a lovely beech wood, and supported the claim that it was second only to Burnham Beeches in the south. Traditionally it has been regarded as the last surviving stretch of the Great North Wood between the Downs and London. In 1921 it was known as Purley Common but it fell into private hands and a sale for housing purposes was imminent. The Parish Council and the local residents, ably concerted by Capt Carpenter DSO RN, secured its retention as a common by paying off a loan with a 2d local rate. After its acquisition, the Parish Council fired a rocket. In 1944 one of the first V2 rockets fell there.

Purley Downs Golf Club has been operating from its downland site since 1894. Originally the downs were used by local farmers for keeping sheep and by others for rifle practice. In the early years of the golf club, members played around the sheep, as agreed with the local farmer. They teed off from sand-boxes and used a wooden hut for a club-house. Judiciously the farmer from Purley Oaks Farm, Thomas Chandler, appeared to have been a member in 1901. Between 1914 and 1927, Purley Downs Halt was the club members' exclusive station and they also enjoyed reduced fares when travelling there. In 1933 the great Henry Cotton played in the professional golf tournament at Purley Downs Golf Club.

In 1960, local amateur actors rehearsed a performance of *Twelfth Night* in the garden of Hill Barn, Purley Downs Road. Hill Barn was one of a number of distinguished residences demolished in 1978 to make room for housing development.

Charles J. Oxenham was a tenant farmer on Pace's Farm, Riddlesdown, when these farm workers posed in about 1913 before their annual outing. The Oxted railway line passed through the Riddlesdown farms. The tenant farmers lost their farms when the owners sold them to Laing's for housing development (See page 27).

In October 1917, two young boys play in Downscourt Road, looking north to the site of Mitchley Avenue.

Douglas Oxenham took this photograph of his wife, Violet, c. 1947, standing by his Triumph Dolomite, before the Mitchley estate was developed on land which his father had farmed. Mitchley was one of the ancient names of a farm field.

Stone axes from the Stone Age or Neolithic Age have been found on Riddlesdown Common, which was also renowned for its Pyramidal, Great Butterfly and Man Orchids. The common, shown here in about 1914, had been purchased bit by bit in the nineteenth century by the City of London, including land bought from Frank Wigsell Arkwright of Purley Bury House (See page 66). A visit to Riddlesdown usually included a visit to Gardner's Pleasure Resort. This was opened in 1883 and its attractions included a miniature railway, donkeys, aviaries, a monkey house and, of course, its tea rooms. A macabre feature was the graves of animals which had provided the rides and the grave of a pet creature belonging to survivors from the Boer War. Sunday school trips continued there until the 1920s but the site was sold for building in 1934.

Instead of making further extensions to All Saints' Church in the 1950s, it was decided to provide daughter churches. St Anthony's Church was opened in Hamsey Green in 1957. Here at Riddlesdown, the foundation stone of St Edmund's Church Hall was laid on 25 September 1954 by the Rector of Sanderstead, the Revd Clifton Wolters.

St Edmund's Church Hall was designed to act jointly as a place of worship and social gathering. On 28 September 1957, a church fair was held which obviously involved a large number of the local community.

Five

Sanderstead: From Railway Bridge to Crossroads

In the 1920s, it was considered a great pleasure to enter the new world that appeared when passing under the railway bridge in Sanderstead Road. There were new villas to admire on the way to the countryside. To the right of the bridge there was a cart track that led to 150 allotments whose owners had to belong to 'the labouring population'. In 1884, as the new estates below the station were being constructed, an extensive Saxon burial site was discovered. Skeletons, iron knives and a small pottery vase were found. In 1902 John Kendall, who was building a large estate off Sanderstead Road, suggested the name of his daughter Florence for a road. His home town, Penwortham in Lancashire, also served as the name of a new road. Subsequently he used other names from his family including Edgar and Victoria. In 1905 there were 1,660 residents in 342 houses in Sanderstead. By 1911 the population had increased to 2,853 in 628 houses. The new residents enjoyed recently supplied amenities. The East Surrey Water Co. began to supply water in 1897 and gas and electricity were used in local houses from 1906.

This postcard, dated 1914, shows Station Parade looking very much as it does today although the large houses opposite, designed by James Williams (see page 85), are no longer there. Even the names that appear on the shops in this picture still have a familiar ring, like Bowditch and Grant, Hooker and Rogers and Hall & Co. The open wooden gates, by which carts of coal merchants and carriages entered the station forecourt, were lockable at nights and at weekends.

Although this postcard is dated 1936, the photograph is more likely to have been taken in the late 1920s, judging by the vehicles. The only shop in Sanderstead in 1899 was Frosel's village store and post office in Sanderstead Village by the school. Alfred Lye, stores and post office, was the first to open in Station Parade in 1902. Parker & Sons, butchers, opened in 1907. G. Aubrey, newsagent, H. Harrison, fishmonger, and Morgan & Sons, fruiterers, joined them in 1908. In 1910 some of the shops in the parade were still under construction. Makepeace, whose name still appears over the present pharmacy, replaced J.W. Wood, Chemist. By 1912 all the shops were occupied. In 1997 some ill-conceived parking regulations may reverse the last statement.

This may have been the occasion when Mrs Cowdrey of the White House and Mrs Small, the village headmistress, were returning from a London hospital after collecting callipers for a poor, local, crippled boy. When their train reached Sanderstead they would have rung a bell outside the station. This would have alerted the fly proprietor and cabman either at his home in Glossop Road or at his shop at 8 Station Parade. His was the only means of transport to the village before the 1920s.

Sanderstead station was opened on 10 March 1884, after the intended line had remained incomplete for twenty years. It might have been a main line station if the original design to build Oxted to Brighton and Oxted to Dover lines had been implemented. The opening of the line coincided with the building of Glossop Road and Broomhall Road. The 1933 Morris car indicates that this was a scene in front of the old station in the late 1930s.

Around 1918, Sanderstead station had a large bookstall and staff which older residents may recall. Younger ones will remember Mrs Martin's sweet kiosk by the down platform. Inside the booking hall there used to be a newspaper shop, which in 1997 became a coffee and snack bar.

In 1942, a bomb failed to do as much damage to the timber-clad station as the fire of June 1986. Railway officials arrived to assess the damage.

A 1935 aerial view of Sanderstead shows traffic moving along Mayfield Road. St Anne's College occupied a major position on the map, opposite to a large corner-house, Beech House. Purley Oaks Road may be seen with St Mary's Church (1926) and the Memorial Hall (1922).

In 1909, the Convent of the Ladies of Mary opened St Anne's College, in response to a concern about the lack of Catholic teaching in the district. As a lure to overseas students it was stated in the prospectus that the school was within walking distance of Croydon airport. In 1939, ninety pupils were evacuated to Hatchlands, East Clandon, now a National Trust property. When flying bombs fell perilously close to the school in 1944, pupils were evacuated to Dunblane in Perthshire. The school's Golden Jubilee was celebrated in 1959 with a performance of *The Happiest Days of Your Life*.

Some of the pupils of the school went on an outing to Box Hill on 17 March 1926. They were Maggie Samprell, Margery Peacock, Jessie Scard, Kitty Ellison, Betty Imrie and Nancy Privett. Of course, school uniform had to be worn, even on an excursion. Grant's was the official school suppliers. At the time a blue serge tunic with St Anne's badge and figured girdle cost just over £1. The school blazer cost between 15 shillings and 19 shillings (75p to 95p). Jewellery was not permitted!

The basis of the school's curriculum was Christian doctrine but a full range of subjects was taught, including mathematics, languages and sciences. The school was not only academic but offered a practical secretarial course, physical education and organised games. Fencing was one of those games in 1925, as shown here. The fees for all of the academic instruction and extra-curricular activities were less than £6 a term in 1937, which included books and materials. Boarders paid just over £20 a term.

In the early 1950s, the school gave a performance of *The Scarlet Pimpernel*. Among local pupils taking part were Kate Beckley, Sue White, Ann Delaney, Diana Mount and Anne Gravestock.

Pupils from the school also visited Box Hill in the 1950s. Some names of the girls recalled are: Jennifer Smith, Ann White, June Powell, Jean Box, Geraldine Baker, Ann Rimer, Joan Pearce, Diana Clements, Teresa Purnell, Catherine Byrne, Anna Barnes, Judith Read, Mary Thelwell, Diana Jones and Diana Ralston.

St Anne's College, Sanderstead, in 1953, the year of the Coronation of Queen Elizabeth II.

The St Anne's College choir, under their conductor, Miss Bunt, sang at the Albert Hall during the Lourdes Centenary celebrations, 19 February 1958.

In 1977, St Anne's College merged into Coloma School and moved to Coloma's new site at Shirley. The former pupils' association of St Anne's held its last meeting in the school in October 1980. Demolition began on 21 November in the same year.

Beech House, 4 November 1936, stood proudly on the opposite side of Sanderstead Road to St Anne's College. It was a fitting residence to match those houses east of Beechwood Road, which had been designed by James Williams, a Quaker and a local resident. He based his designs on old Surrey farmhouses. With his partner, Davey, he restored Penshurst Place. However, the sheer magnificence and grand position of Beech House made it a local landmark. In 1913 the site was designated for building purposes. By 1915 its first owner's name, Fred Hanscomb, and the name of Beech House appeared in the local directory. In the mid-1920s William Dunkin was the owner, but in 1932 it lay unoccupied. Then, in about 1933, Dr Woolrich moved from 9 Beechwood Road into Beech House. Fortunately it escaped major war damage but, in the late 1980s, was gutted by fire after being empty for a long time. A conversion to a block of flats has retained many of the original features.

Dr Woolrich in the middle of a group of members of Sanderstead Dramatic Club at an annual dinner. He became its President in 1939 and his wife, holding a bouquet, stands next to him. His family had moved to Sanderstead in 1896 and his father volunteered to manage the war relief fund in the First World War for the Parish Council. Dr Woolrich spent the war years in the RAMC after an education at Whitgift School and St John's College, Cambridge. In 1920 he joined Dr Everington in a general medical practice, in which he served for thirty-seven years. He was also, for twenty-six years, the appointed anaesthetist for Croydon and Purley Hospitals.

It was only possible to travel on foot through West Hill to anywhere around Sanderstead after the night of the 'hurricane', 16 October 1987. During the night over half a million trees were lost in Surrey alone. A motorist was killed in South Croydon.

Airplane Crash at Sanderstead

This is not a wartime scene! In about 1928 a film was being made about the First World War. A 'German' aircraft took off from Croydon airport and crashed into a house near the pathway between East and West Hill.

Haymaking in Britain Field, Briton Hill Farm in 1917. The chalky soil in Sanderstead was poor for crops but it was good for turf and sheep farming. Briton Hill Farm, known also locally as Stobbart's Farm (from about 1925), was one of the leading eight farms in the area although not as large as Purley Farm or the Home Farm of Sanderstead Court. In the district there was little arable farming, which had reached a peak by 1843 when additional land for ploughing had been obtained by encroaching on woods and wastelands.

An Iron Age track was said to pass through Briton Hill Farm and continue up Sanderstead Hill (formerly Briton Hill). Saxon burial fields had also been found on the farm. Until 1931 carts loaded high with hay regularly passed along Briton Hill Road. The entrance to the farm nurseries was between 42 and 44 Briton Hill Road and the farmhouse was at No. 28. Joyce Eeles, who had lived in the road in the 1920s, recalled that most houses had live-in maids. Bread and milk were delivered by horse and cart but Sainsbury's carried ordered groceries by motor van.

Members of the 18th Purley Scouts took part in this cowboy event in 1961 as a change from their usual routines.

The 18th Purley Scouts were formed in Sanderstead in 1937. In 1987 they celebrated their Golden Jubilee when a founder member cut the celebratory cake.

Some of the founder members also endeavoured to get down and practise once again their childhood rituals – but on this occasion, with more difficulty.

A sweet gum tree was planted in the grounds of Sanderstead Library on 14 April 1951 to commemorate the Festival of Britain.

The sign pointing towards Purley Downs Road, c. 1923. A telegraph pole stands tall in Miller's Farm where rhubarb and cabbages were a speciality. A lone single-decker bus struggles up Sanderstead Hill. In the early years buses carried blocks to put behind the wheels when there was a fear of slipping back down the hill. In 1921 the first bus service, S4, ran at two-hour intervals from the Red Deer to Edenbridge via Sanderstead and Warlingham. It would stop wherever anyone hailed it. After much opposition a bus took a route along Mayfield Road.

On 29 December 1984, Mrs Martha Rosier, Sanderstead's oldest resident, celebrated her 103rd birthday. She was renowned locally as an excellent cook and as mother of Ellen Rosie (See pages 112 and 113).

Six

Church and Manor

Church Lane, a narrow track, was a
main route to Croydon for Sanderstead
residents until the 1920s. When
returning from Croydon the church
lych gate in Addington Road must
have been a welcome site for travellers
from 1905 at the end of the lane.
Church Lane was quite uninhabited
until Malcolm Grahame went to live
at Little Langley in 1926. By 1928 on
the left side there were three residences,
three unoccupied new houses and
three houses under construction. On
the opposite side only T. Ibbetson was
resident at Fieldgate. Today it is a major
thoroughfare with many houses.

All Saints' Church, Sanderstead, c. 1797-1800, as depicted in a water colour sketch by Henry Petrie FSA. He was the son of a Streatham dancing master, his own intended profession, and an antiquary as well as an artist. His patrons included the Earl Spencer. Around 1800, he undertook a survey of churches in southern England. The church was built in about 1230 AD, although there was some tentative evidence of a previous church. There were burials there before the thirteenth century. Roman cement and pieces of Saxon tomb were discernible in the building of the present church. The earliest part of the building is past the eastern arch on the north side where an early piscina is situated.

This was a view of the east end of All Saints' Church, witnessed by G. Yates as he recorded it in water colours. The box pews were painted light brown and red plush covered the altar, lectern and pulpit. The church was in poor repair at the time and, in 1826, a minstrel's gallery on a balcony was removed. In 1832 the original windows were replaced. G. Yates was not Gideon Yates of Lancaster, but the artist who produced a series of views of London bridges from 1827-1837. Examples of his work are to be found in the British Museum, the Guildhall and in other London museums.

Plans were drawn up for the extension of the church in 1938. In the reign of George III there were only 33 houses and a population of 204 in Sanderstead. The ancient church seated between 150 and 200. From 1921 to 1931 the actual number of parishioners had increased from 477 to 2,095. The plans have been only partially implemented as there has not been an expansion to the west side of the church. Wartime damage from incendiaries necessitated the renovation of the spire, towards which the Queen Mother made a donation in memory of her great-grandmother, Mrs Oswald Smith, related by marriage to the Smiths of Selsdon Park, who had lived in Sanderstead in the early nineteenth century.

This postcard of All Saints' Church, dated 1902, was sent by sea mail (Paquebot) to Rawalpindi. The postcard itself pre-dates 1902. Before that year only the address was allowed on the reverse and, as here, the message had to be written on the picture side. In 1902 the lych gate was in its original position on the pond side of the church.

There were three fine yew trees in the churchyard of All Saints'. This one was near the present entrance to the churchyard from the car park. A stump is all that remains of it. Mr Hobson, taking part in a photographic survey of Surrey, recorded this tree in about 1899. The contemporary Croydon Microscopical and Natural History Club thought that it was 500 years old.

The hurricane of October 1987 brought down this cedar tree across the stump of the ancient yew. A disconsolate churchwarden surveys the damage.

On 6 April the *Croydon Advertiser* reported that a 'religious' fanatic had run amok through the graveyard. About 100 gravestones were damaged, mostly crosses and angels. About thirty parishioners helped the Rector, Canon Colin Scott (now Bishop of Hulme in Manchester), to clear the mess. Many hours were spent in cementing the stones, although some were beyond repair.

In November 1982, Canon Scott invited Joan Landreth, wife of the former Rector, Canon Derek Landreth, to open the church's Autumn Fair. Although having suffered a stroke which left her without speech, she was determined to open the event by holding aloft a large card bearing the message, 'Get on with it!' Traditionally the proceeds from this fair go to needy local charities and not to the church. Parishioners have a long history of giving. On 5 September 1658 a collection of 16s 1d (about 80p) was sent to the people of Wapping distressed by a blast of gunpowder.

The near unification of church and manor. Ellen Rosier remembered walking from the village road through a primrose wood to the pond. Beyond there was a ditch by the church to prevent the cows making their way to Sanderstead Court.

In July 1980, Mr Atwood of Belmont, California, a direct descendant of the Atwood family who were Lords of the Manor, cut a cake celebrating the 750th Anniversary of All Saints' Church at a party in the Rectory garden. The anniversary was marked by the St Catherine's aisle extension to the church.

Rubbings from the family brasses of John and Diones Atwood and their ten children. The inscription reads: 'Of your piety pray for the souls of John A'wodde and Diones his wife which John deceased on 30th July 1525, on whose souls Jesus have mercy.' A chancery suit of 1547 stated that Nicholas Atwood was heir to Sanderstead Manor and the last male owner with Atwood blood died in 1795. American relatives derive their ancestry from Harman Atwood of Boston, and the grandson of Nicholas and Olive. The Atwood arms consist of a lion rampant between three acorns, crest, arm erect holding battleaxe.

1599   Johannes Batten filius Rutoni Batten ...
      Maria Styntt filia Thome Styntt ...

1600   Anna Ownstead filia Henrey Ownst ...
      Ownstead wood filius Harmanni wood ... 19 ...
      Johannes Batten filius Antonij Batten ...

1602   Anna Heath filia Roberti Heath ...
      Johannes Ownstead filius Henrick Ownstead ...
      Chris wood filia Harmanni woode ...
      William ... filius ... ...

1603   Elizabeth Batten filia Antonij Batten ...
      Elizabeth Woodstock filia John Woodstock ...

1604   ... Busse filia Nicolai Busse ...
      Anna Atwood filia Harmanni Atwood ...
      Anne Bridger filia Henrici Bridger ...
      Anne Ownstead filia Georgij Ownstead ...

1605   Anna Woodstock filia John Woodstock ...

1606   Susanna Atwood filia Harmanni Atwood ...
      Elizabeth Ownstead filia ...
      Georgij Ownstead ...
      Atwood Ownstead filius Henrici ...

Above: Some of the church records were displayed in the church in 1983. Details in the baptismal registers include the births of Anna Ownstead in 1600 and Anna Atwood in 1604. Other parish records recorded the baptism of James, the black slave of Mr St John, in 1772, and the drowning of the parish clerk, Robert Rutter in a pond in Addington in 1802.

Left: All Saints' Church is rich in brasses and memorials. John Ownstead, who died in 1600, was 'Master of Her Most Dread Majesties Horse for Forty Years' (Queen Elizabeth I). He left a third of the manor to his sister and a third to Harman Atwood, who acquired the lot in 1653.

This memorial bears the Mellish arms and is most likely in memory of George Mellish who died in 1693. His gravestone is on the north side of the central aisle. Robert Mellish, who died in 1627, was the owner of Lymes Place or the Place House, the gentleman's house of the manor. Sanderstead Court was the home of yeomen farmers.

The monument to Mary (Maria) Audley, who died in 1655, was originally placed east to west but was moved to its present position in about 1837. It blocks the south aisle so that only one side of this favourite monument is visible. Mary was the daughter of Matthew Bedell and the widow of Ralph Hawtree. She later married Lewis Audley, a Commonwealth JP, who was authorised to marry couples at his home, Purley Bury House.

In 1676, Harman Atwood built Sanderstead Court and his initials 'HA' appeared above the doorway. Materials from a former house were used in making Place House. The last squire was Wigsell Arkwright who sold the estate in 1919.

Mrs Morton, the wife of the tenant of Sanderstead Court, took this photograph in 1912. Her husband was Mr E. Morton of 'Morton's pickles'. Every year the Mortons gave all the children of the district an entertainment and presents from a gigantic Christmas tree. The liveried servants waited on the children and in the evening local adults were invited to the Court for an entertainment by London theatricals. Mr Morton often appeared in the village driving a high dog cart in tandem with two Dalmatian dogs. In about 1928 the Court became an annexe to Selsdon Park Hotel but during its occupancy by the War Office in 1944 it was burnt down and finally demolished in 1958.

When Sanderstead Court became a hotel, its name was changed to Selsdon Court. The hotel's brochure said that this room was the Virgin Queen's favourite room when staying in Sanderstead, although the Court was not built until long after her death.

After the demolition of the Court, a number of outhouses remained, including the golf club-house. The clock tower and stable block above were pulled down in 1979.

Left: The annual United Procession of Witness by Sanderstead churches, Good Friday 1987. A short service was held in the grounds of each denominational church. Here the procession is just passing the Methodist Church.

Below: In the 1987 Procession of Witness, Father John Hartley and Canon Tom Smail converse as the procession moves towards the Roman Catholic Church of the Holy Family. New churches opened to meet the needs of a growing population. The Congregational (URC) Church opened in 1939 and during 1956 and 1957, the Holy Family, the Methodist Church and the Brethren Meeting Place (Mitchley Chapel) all opened.

Seven

Sanderstead: From the Pond to Hamsey Green

An aerial photograph of Sanderstead taken in 1935 still shows the rural nature of the locality. Sanderstead Plantation dominates Addington Road and in 'Lower' Sanderstead, farmlands are the main feature. From the crossroads a pathway by a large pond leads to the church and the manor house to its rear. Shops along the Limpsfield Road opposite to the village school have arrived; Gwen Barry, hairdresser, Killick, news and tobacco, Scotts' confectionery and teas, and the Corner Cafe have all opened. Much of Sanderstead's charm remains. The observation of William Cobbett (1763-1835) that Sanderstead dwellers got up at earliest dawn and repaired with cheerfulness to their several occupations remains pertinent to today's commuting villagers.

A lone farmer with his shire horses ploughs Rogers Field, which ran between Limpsfield Road and Sanderstead Wood, in 1916. Pastoral scenes like this were common before the housing development of the 1930s. When looking at the development of the area there should always be an awareness of the countryside that has been replaced.

In 1978 Celia Lamont Jones planted the first of seventy-five roses on the roundabout in double celebration of Queen Elizabeth II's Silver Jubilee and the 50th Anniversary of the Sanderstead Residents' Association, of which she was President and which is still serving the community today.

Canon John Morris, the Rector, dedicated a memorial plaque in 1967 commemorating Tom Sherlock's unique contribution to Sanderstead village life. The Sanderstead Preservation Society had inaugurated the fund, which also provided for a new water supply to the pond and seats and trees around it. Godfrey Talbot presided over the event and gave a talk on the history of the Manor (See page 6).

In 1904, H.V. Irwin of Uplands, Sanderstead, took this photograph of the Old Rectory. There was a stone over the house bearing the initials 'OA' for Olive Atwood, sister of the Harman Atwood who built Sanderstead Court in 1676. She had the Rectory constructed in 1680. It ceased to be used as a rectory in 1928 and was demolished in 1962.

Local people call the field beyond the footpath by the pond, the 'Gruffy'. It is the nearest Sanderstead comes to having a village green. Village fairs, community hymn singing and other local events are held there. Its existence has been threatened in favour of a cottage hospital, now a defunct idea, or a car park. The Residents' Association keeps a watchful eye on Sanderstead's heritage.

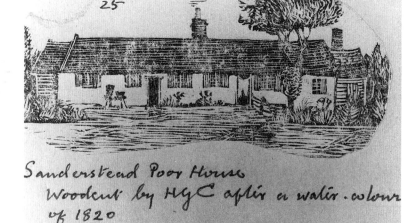

Sanderstead Poor House
Woodcut by HgC after a water-colour
of 1820

Harry G. Carter OBE, antiquarian, typographer and translator, produced this woodcut from a water colour by J. Hassell, which is in the British Museum. It shows the Sanderstead Poor House, probably among the houses set around the 'village green' area. It was an essential for the village, as a 1598 statute required every parish to have a poor house.

On an 1868 Ordnance Survey map, several cottages were shown opposite the White House. This 1851 sketch by an, as yet, unidentified artist shows one of those buildings that possibly was in use as a private school.

A map of 1865 showed that there was a well between the pond and the church, further supporting speculation that here had been a village green. The area was enclosed in 1799 by the Lord of the Manor who bought and demolished six cottages, which were replaced by wooden buildings along the village road. This cottage, photographed by J.C. Stenning in 1874, was one of those remaining and may have been the one used as a schoolroom in 1873 during the building of the first village school.

A cricket match between a Surrey XI and a Kent XI was recorded at Sanderstead Common on 8 September 1731. It is believed that organised cricket began in Sanderstead in 1881. The first captain was Samuel Cowdrey, great grandfather of Colin Cowdrey, who was the manorial estate manager living at the White House. T.P. Sherlock was captain in 1906 and maintained a lifelong association with the Sanderstead Club as player, friend and benefactor. In 1910 the team comprised, back row, from left to right: Davis, Hew, Chapman, Sylvester and Sherlock (T.W.). Centre row: Capt Carpenter RN, Sherlock (T.P.), Cowdrey (S) and Sherlock (W.G.). Front row: Bate, Rew and Roll.

By 1925, Sanderstead Cricket Club had left the Recreation Ground to play at 'Sherlock's Field', later called the 'Old Sawmill Field', which had been presented to the village as a trust by Tom Sherlock. In the 1930s the team included, back row, from left to right: A. Imrie, R. Turnbull, (?), N. Brown, Woodward, 'Unkel' Goldby, H. Imrie. Front row: N. Wilkinson, J. Turnbull, Holt, Tom Sherlock, May, J. Wilkinson.

Sanderstead Club cricketers in their 1981 Centenary Year. Back row, from left to right: Eccles, Gord, Harrison, Haynes, P. Brown (captain), O'Sullivan, H. Sherlock, A. Witchell, D. Dennis. Front row: Mathews, Corderoy, Chatham, I. Witchell (vice captain), Harding (scorer) and Eastwood.

Other sporting clubs have arisen from time to time but photographs from their archives have not emerged. In 1949 W.F. Wood of Field Close was the Hon. Sec. of Sanderstead United FC. There used to be a Sanderstead Athletics Club. Above is a pre-war Sanderstead Hill Cricket Club. Some of the players identified are Dick Townley, front row right, who had sports shops in Station Parade and in Cranleigh Parade, and Teddy Townley, his brother, who is seated at the front with a score book. To the left of Dick Townley is Jack White and to his left is Pere Herbert in sports jacket and flannels; the next player is unknown, but to his left are Freddie Shearing, Phil Naish and Kenneth Herbert. In the back row, second from the right, is Bob White.

The White House may have been built about 1550 as 'Copthawe' or 'Coppyd Halle' and associated with Robert Mellish. The name White House may have been derived from John White who appeared in the rent rolls of 1450. According to tradition the cellar was used for storing smuggled brandy and there was a secret passage to Sanderstead Court. In the nineteenth century, the White House was known as Whitehouse Farm until the farm buildings were destroyed by fire. Sir Bertram Jones was the owner from 1932 and Lady Jones presented cups to the Sanderstead Horse Show on Barrows Field (now the Recreation Ground). Douglas Oxenham won a prize for the horse with the longest tail!

Ellen Rosier sat at the front of a group of people invited by Mr and Mrs Jasper Nicholls to their White House garden. They were the owners from about 1913 to about 1927. Ellen went with Mr Nicholls to obtain a donkey from Stobbart's Farm (Briton Hill) to pull the lawn mower. The donkey refused!

In Sanderstead Village in 1909 the village school and the post office were on the right, but on the left there were only fields of cows.

The village changed little between 1900 and 1920. The village school's bell-tower may be seen on the left. The school opened in 1875 on land donated by Colonel Wigsell. There were twenty-five boys and thirty-three girls initially in the school who each paid one (old) penny a week. The wooden fence maker in the district must have been very much in demand. On the left there were fences around Beechview Cottages (see page 118), the school and in front of the fields going towards the White House. On the right there was a long fence securing the cattle in fields where the shops now stand.

Mrs Small, Ellen Rosier's great aunt, was headmistress of the village school from about 1895 to 1924. In 1919 she invited Ellen to take part in a peace pageant – she is the child whose hat is marked with a cross. Ellen has recalled this period in the life of Sanderstead when there were few cottages along the road to Hamsey Green. The village was beautiful with May trees and laburnums as she walked to Borough Grange Farm to collect the milk in her own churn. The lamplighter put out his last lamp outside the school-house.

Miss Hilda Bird was the headmistress of the village school from 1925 to about 1929. She is shown here with her assistant, Miss Toynbee. A former pupil at school in 1926 has recalled that Miss Bird and Miss Lancaster taught all the subjects between them to the children aged between 7 and 14.

Children in the upper part of the school in 1920. They would have been at the school in 1918 when complaints were made to the local wartime aerodromes about machine gun practice near the school and the target practice on Miller's field.

A class of infants in the early 1920s. Mrs Small was the headteacher. At lunchtime, at her own expense, she provided hot soup and milk to supplement the bread lunch of the children of poor farm labourers. The school was forced to close on a number of occasions: in 1905, poor drainage causing sore throats; in 1907, whooping cough; in 1913, measles; in 1920, scarlet fever and in 1922, influenza. It was closed between 1931 and 1933 because there were insufficient pupils.

The staff of the 'new' school, now called Gresham, in 1976. Back row, from left to right: Mrs Hayes, Mrs Walpole, Miss Jennings, Miss Judd, Mrs Fairbrother. Front row: Mrs Seaman, Mr Gerrard, Mrs Bone (headteacher), Mr Rees, Mrs Mason. The new parts of the school had been built between 1936 and 1938. In 1940 there were two unexploded bombs on the school, one of which blew up. Constant air raids were recorded and some children were evacuated to North Wales and others went to Leeds. After the war the school adopted the name 'Gresham'. The title was adopted from John Gresham, who received Sanderstead Manor from Henry VIII after the Dissolution of the Monasteries (See page 41).

In 1979, the Year of the Child, Betty Bloom of Cullen's Store invited children from Gresham School to perform country dances outside the shop. (By kind permission of the *Advertiser* Group)

Junior children from Gresham School performed a version of *Cinderella*, written by teacher Mr Lockyer, in December 1983.

Children from Ridgeway and Gresham Junior Schools replaced trees destroyed by the 1987 and 1989 storms (See page 86). (By kind permission of the *Advertiser* Group)

In 1906, this group of labourers pumped water outside the old village school.

Dipsley's Field, 5 August 1935, again showing the pervading rural aspect of Sanderstead. Dipsley's Field and Dipsley's Shaw adjoined Riddlesdown Farm from which there were footpaths leading to the old Rectory and Miller's Field and also to the smithy and Borough Farm.

At the beginning of the First World War in 1914, Sanderstead boy scouts, preparing to make their wartime contribution, lined up outside the village school.

Some twenty-five years later, before a second world conflict, the Revd Howard Rose, Rector, posed with scouts, guides, brownies and cubs in the Rectory garden. Among those who have been recognised are: Eric Bishop, Joan Bishop, Joan Pearson, Joan Everitt, Ellen Rosier and Tony Bateman, a future village butcher. Much development in Sanderstead occurred between 1934 and 1936 so that the appointment of the Revd Howard Rose in 1935 was timely. Under his leadership church activities greatly increased, the church building was enlarged and young people were encouraged in their endeavours.

Above: In 1920 Mrs Leppard posed outside her general store, off licence and post office. Her husband had been the Parish Clerk from the 1890s when James Frosel and his wife kept the post office. The village children regarded Mrs Frosel as a witch. More recent owners included Joseph Smith, Smith and Allison, Miss Allison and Cullens. Cullens maintained the period frontage but subsequent developments have lost the charm of the old building.

In 1930, Borough Farm became
Bowerman's Dairy and in 1932, Frederick
King's Dairy. The farm house, Borough
Grange, a little brick and flint building,
had probably been built by Harman
Atwood II as a home farm for the new
Sanderstead Court. In 1890 Wilson
was the tenant. He bred thoroughbred
carthorses at £2,000 each. During the
General Strike in 1926, Hall's the coal
merchants turned out over a hundred of
their horses to graze on the farm. In 1937
Capt T.S. Sturley Clutter MC had his
riding school there. Reduced fees were
offered to pupils at St Anne's College.

Right: Looking towards Croydon,
Borough Farm is on the right in this 1932
photograph. Limpsfield Road had still
to wait a few years before the road was
widened.

Opposite below: Although this postcard
showing the eighteenth century
Beechview Cottages is postmarked
1957, it is more likely to be a view some
thirty years earlier, before the many-
armed telegraph poles were fortunately
replaced by underground wires. Here
in 1920, beyond Beechview Cottages,
was the James Brand Memorial Hall,
where the villagers held meetings and
the occasional social event. Mr Revill,
later a Croydon councillor, lived at the
Gables. Beyond were only Ivy Cottages,
Rose Cottages and Old Police Station
Cottages before Hamsey Green.

In the 1920s, the road to Hamsey Green was still aptly termed Sanderstead Village. The large house in the centre is the Gables, built in 1908 and now called Barrowsfield. In the foreground, the four cottages on the left, Ivy Cottages, still bear the arms of the Atwood family. Just past the cottages was a public footpath to Hamsey Green and Court Farm. The two finger posts, pointing to a footpath across farmland to Riddlesdown Farm and to Kenley Station, were taken down in 1898 by Borough Farm who objected to public use across its land. A 'permissive footpath' was established when the Commons Preservation Society compromised by dropping its claim to an established public footpath between the Rectory and the White House.

The Old Forge smithy stood alone in 1900. When Atwood Wigsell added the eighteenth-century building to his estate, he placed on a gable his initials, 'AW', which remain there today. Thomas Dulake, blacksmith, took over from a smith who had used the premises for illicit beer-making for the local folk. Charles Bale, who took over in 1910, was the last working blacksmith there. From 1924, Fred Beard, a retired doctor, lived at the smithy until Miss Richardson and Miss Cox took it over as the 'Skep' for a school. They let local Roman Catholics use the schoolroom for services from 1942. The building is still in use as a church hall.

On 5 September 1958, a few doors away from the Old Forge, at 121 Limpsfield Road, a heavy downpour brought flooding. All hands were required to deal with it, including the rescue of a motor cycle.

Len and Douglas Oxenham and Albert Colebrook had permission in 1938 to remove the hay from the field between Lime Meadow Avenue and Limpsfield Road, to their stables (See pages 27 and 72).

This 1970 aerial view over Limpsfield Road shows, in the left foreground, the Methodist Church and Atwood School, still with its hut-classrooms. Opposite to Mitchley Hill is the fire station which, in 1997, is undergoing demolition.

Bluebells abounded in this favourite Sanderstead walking area around 1937. There are fewer trees now since the army cleared some in the Second World War and the Great Storm cleared others. In 1823 these woodlands (now Kings Wood) were known as Sanderstead Wood and Kings Wood was a small wood north of Kingswood Lodge. In 1955, Roger Little and other Bourne Society members discovered a Roman 'village' of about 100 AD. Pottery fragments, a military spear and Samianware were found there.

Right: In 1932, when there was sewer digging between Downs Court Road and Mitchley Avenue, these small bronze coins of Constantine and Crispus were found. They were minted in London in 320 AD.

Below: In the late 1980s, when a new playground and buildings were being constructed for Atwood G.M. Primary School, Gillian Batchelor and other London Museum archaeologists and volunteers worked swiftly to unearth an extensive area of Roman occupation. Some 5,000 pieces of first and second century pieces of pottery and other artefacts were found on this Iron age (500 BC–200 AD) Romano-British site. (Photo: Mrs J. Hill, Deputy Head)

The children here, c. 1966, were among the first pupils to enter Atwood School on or soon after 13 June 1960 with Mrs Beryl Cutts in charge. They were then in their final year before secondary school. Back row, from left to right: Mr McLeod, Kelly, Thomas, Coe, Reilly, Wade, Mortimer, Barnes, Hillier, Mr A.D. Bolwell (headteacher). Third row: Francis, Fitt, Gell, Harris, Legg, Pratt, Edmunds, Constable, Eayres, Taylor, Smith. Second row: Fellowes, Floodgate, Gray, Laver, Miller, Shrives, Smith, Hayler, Lee, Innes, Batley. Front row: Bashford, West, McCallum, Saxby, Rimmer, Rotter.

The Atwood School staff posed for a photograph in June 1967. Back row: Mrs Leedon, Mrs Mustchin, Mrs Rimmer, Mrs Blewett, Mr McLeod, Mrs High, Miss Henry, Mrs Dutton, Mr Elton. Front row: Mrs Routley, Mrs Philpott, Miss Dickens, Mr Bolwell, Mrs Poulton, Mrs Gossage, Mrs Wheeler.

Above: Limpsfield Road near Hamsey Green was comparatively deserted in 1925 as a single vehicle approaches from Sanderstead. The Limpsfield Trust had made the only previous developments to the road. After the Napoleonic wars it used unemployed men and men on poor relief to carry out the maintenance of the road. Some of the money for the work came from a toll-booth near Hamsey Green pond from about 1828.

Right: In the 1920s, the pond was much larger than today; large enough to accept a horse and cart for cooling down. Originally the pond was called Wychmere (White Pond) and was one of the Sanderstead-Warlingham boundary markers that was often in dispute.

Nancy Privett and her family have been selected as representative of other families who have found contentment living in the area across generations. The name of Privett appeared among the pioneers of modern Sanderstead who went to live in the newly-built Penwortham Road, Purley. At that time anything which included the name Purley, such as Purley Bury, Purley Oaks or Purley Farm, was in the parish of Sanderstead. When Nancy was born in 1910 there were only about 2,500 people in Sanderstead. She was well respected locally as a dance teacher but she also held dances at the prestigious Waldorf Hotel. It was as Nancy or 'Girlie' White that she was best known, and she was an outstanding amateur actress with Sanderstead Dramatic Club, who enthralled audiences over many years. She spent the whole of her 86 years living in Sanderstead.

Nancy Privett married Jack White at St Gertrude's Roman Catholic Church, South Croydon. The best man, on her right, is Bob White. The two White brothers were both members of a Sanderstead cricket team (See page 109). Other local people pictured are Molly Betts and Ann, Jill and Wendy Privett.

Nancy at her daughter's wedding at All Saints' Church, Sanderstead, in 1963. From left to right: John Rudolph, Diana Abbott, George Fullard (bridegroom), Suzanne White (bride), Nancy ('Girlie') White and Jack White. In the front are Lesley White and Heather Banderet.

Although not pictured here, Nancy also attended her granddaughter's wedding at All Saints' Church in 1994. From left to right: Sandra Fullard, Richard Atkin (bridegroom), Louise Fullard (bride) and parents, Sue and George Fullard.

Acknowledgements

I am indebted to the following:

For writing the introduction, Godfrey Talbot LVO, OBE.

For sharing their enthusiasm by example, Dr Ron Cox, Joy Gadsby, John Gent, Dorothy Tutt, the Bourne Society, Croydon Natural History and Scientific Society.

For inspiration in starting the project, Dorothy Winter.

For providing photographs and help, Freddie Percy (Whitgift Archives); Mrs M. Short (Purley Oaks School); Pam Ward (Croydon Bowling Club); Mr D. Troake (Haling Manor School); Ian Harley (photographs and archives of St John's Church, Selsdon); Mrs Clark (photographs from the Selsdon G.M. Primary School Archives); Selsdon Camera Club: M. Healey, R. Smith, V. Smith, L. Topple, A. Alexander, R. Crump. Ellen Rosier (Sanderstead); Sue Fullard (Dramatic Club, St Anne's College); Harley Sherlock (cricket); Andrew Sherlock; Charles Peyton; Mrs Bartle (Gresham School); Jean Gorvett; Mrs A. Barnes (Sanderstead Junior School); Mrs J. Hill; Sybil Blewett; Althea Woolrich; Pam Shearing; Mrs Raby; Rodney Mander. Riddlesdown/Oxenham family: Vi Oxenham; Dorothy Blackman. Transport: K. Wolstenholme. Computing: Ian Witchell. Predominantly Paper, 200 High Street, Croydon. Croydon Public Libraries: Steve Roud; Oliver Harris and the staffs of Croydon and Purley Local History and Selsdon Libraries for expert help and the use of photographs on pages 25a, 29, 36b, 41, 44a, 56a, 57a, 59a, 60ab, 64b, 66ab, 71b, 72b, 74ab, 84a, 85a, 89b, 94a, 95a, 104b, 105ab, 107b, 118a, 120b, 121a, 122a, 123b. Thanks to Roger Packham and Ted Frith of the Bourne Society for helpful comments on the first edition of this book.

For keeping me going: Dr A. Simonds (National Heart and Chest Hospital) and the physiotherapists of Purley Hospital.

Finally, for supreme tolerance and willingness to help in every way, my wife, Mair.

John B. Gent is an inspiration to everyone who takes an interest in local history. He has written and edited numerous books on the Croydon area including books on transport. He is always ready to support others in their local studies and I am indebted to him for photographs on the following pages: 10a, 19a, 26ab, 28a, 30b, 31ab, 36a, 39ab, 44a, 45b, 56b, 58b, 71a, 78a, 86b, 91, 118b.